Table of Contents

About War

"You busy?" Pat said, looking at Harry, who was sitting next to the potbelly stove in the rear portion of the Smoke House.   He took a sip of coffee before he answered.

"No," Harry said. "Traffic has been down during the day since the 11th." He paused briefly. "I've sold a pile of newspapers and news magazines but this only happens early in the morning and when the evening paper comes in around three."

"You look beat," Harry said looking directly into Pat's eyes.

"I've had some sleepless nights since the planes hit the tower," Pat said, sitting down across from Harry.

"Most people don't know the consequences of what happened on the 11th," Pat said quietly and looked at Harry. Harry nodded.

"You want a cup of coffee Pat?" Harry asked, and Pat shook his head in a negative manner.   There was an eerie silence between the two men.

"How do you tell a young child about war?" Pat asked and looked directly into Harry's eyes.   Harry didn't reply to his question.

"Nancy's grandchild was over at the house looking at cartoons when it came on the television." Pat took a deep breath.   "Little Sally just stood in front of the television set just looking, not moving a muscle." Pat stopped speaking.

"She's only six," Pat said, looking at the floor, "but she knew what was happening."

"She knew real people were being killed in front of her eyes," Pat said while he raised his head to look at Harry.   Harry could see in the man's eyes that Pat was looking for answers and for confirmation that he had done the right thing with this child.

"Nancy came into the room and started to take Sally out, but I motioned her to leave her alone." Pat took another breath.

"The damage had been done," Pat said in a low voice stopping again.

"Her innocence was lost. She'll never be the same. She's been exposed to the horrors that people can do to each other." Pat stopped again and relaxed his body backward into the bamboo rocker and started to rock it backward and forward.

"In a couple of minutes, I took her out to the front porch and down to the barn to show her the new calf that had been born the week before.

"I talked about how happy we were about the new calf while we walked. She was quiet during our walk. I got her to laugh when I told her about my milking a cow when I was a teenager. The cow would hit me with her tail and every minute tries to step on my feet. But even laughing, Sally had a somber look about her. Her look was kind of eerie. I knew she was still thinking about what she had seen just an hour before." Pat said, looking at Harry.

"I spent the rest of the morning with her, taking down to see the ducks at the pond and feeding them before I headed back to the house. I hoped Nancy had turned off all the televisions. She had, and it was time for lunch when we got back to the house. During lunch, Nancy did most of the talking about her daughter and Sally's brother, Eddie. I didn't want to say anything. I had run out of things to talk about to a six-year-old." Pat took a deep breath.

"Nancy took Sally and made her take a nap.

"I was on the front porch in my rocker when she woke up and came out to the porch. She broke me out of my thinking about the devastation and about what would occur in the years ahead."

"'Papa! Papa!'" Sally said. "'What's war?'" she asked in her innocent voice.

"I looked at her. She was looking directly into my eyes. I asked myself how could I explain what war was about and why it had to occur in this world. I could see that her perfect and undisturbed world was about to end.

"I took her on my lap and started to rock.

"I didn't want to answer her question. She was the one that broke the silence. 'Why did all those people have to die?'" she asked in her little voice.

"I still didn't answer her. I didn't know how to explain war. I didn't want to open her blameless world anymore. I thought of Pandora's box. Once it was open, there was no holding back of the evil but in the end, there was hope. The dye had been cast when she had seen this tragic event.

"I told her this: 'War is not nice. It is the worst kind of human behavior. People get hurt who didn't do anything to deserve it,' I said. 'It's like you and your brother when you don't like him. I know that he picks on you at times for no reason. Well, when people get very powerful they try to pick on other people. I know that you don't like him picking on you. I've seen you get really mad at him, and you want to hurt him. Well, this is sort of what war is about.'"

"Oh," she said quickly, getting off my lap. "Granny says were going to town to get some ice cream."

"My rocker stood motionless as this little girl ran inside the house to get Nancy so that we could go to town." Pat stopped and grinned a little.

"You know ice cream heals a lot of wounds in a child." Pat paused briefly. "But her perfect world has ended forever, and no amount of ice cream will heal the knowledge of seeing those people being killed." Pat stopped talking while the rocker became still. Harry nodded.

"You did the best you could," Harry said. "Sally has started on the road to becoming an adult," Harry said, looking directly at Pat.

"War is where we become like our ancestors in the cave," Harry said shaking his head.

"I wish old men would find another way to settle their differences by sending people to kill each other, but this is man's way, not God's---not anyone's God.

"Clang! Clang!" The noise came from the old cowbell on top of the doorframe. Harry got up. Pat looked at his watch.

"I have to go anyway," Pat said. "Nancy's at the dress shop buying Sally a new outfit. She says this will make her forget." The men looked at each other and shook their heads.

Oh," Pat said. "I won't be around for a couple of weeks. You know what the old guys will be talking about." Pat was silent.

"You know how I am about war and killing." He said with a somber expression. Pat thought about the hate that would arise in the coming months and years.

Pat wondered where the line would be drawn between justice and vengeance.

Opening the door to the main street, Pat saw the old Presbyterian church. Both the church and the American flag were at half mast.

Pat just stood there.

"There Jesus throwing out the vendors out of the synagogue' he thought nearly all believers didn't want to deal with this aspect of Christ behavior.....but this was justice, not vengeance.

The Baggataway

He looked down and around at the dead brown grass. The cold wind blew against John's tall, lean frame. The empty space looked like an empty meadow where the grass had been cut before the first snow. The breath John exhaled came out in a white mist.

John moved his head to the left and the right. He could picture the old lacrosse goals on each end of this field.

From the looks of the field, no one had used this place for really anything. Maybe the local kids used it on the weekends as a football field or to play softball, he thought.

He looked again at both ends of the field. This was where they made a bald spot on the field and where a mud puddle would appear after a rain. John smiled. How many years had it been since the last combat between two teams running up and down this field, trying to project and fling a small hard rubber ball into their opponent's goals? How many bones had been broken, how many knees and elbows were made bloody by a dive to secure or throw a small hard rubber object into the clutches of a friendly player's possession or out of the reach of a foe wanting this object at any cost.

John could still imagine the weight of the seasoned oak stick in the grasp of his left hand. He could toss the ball over sixty feet with one swift motion of his hand. His players could only manage a control pitch of twenty feet. At times when luck was with them, they could achieve a pitch and catch of thirty-five feet.

A smile appeared on John's face. He was someone who had seen manhood emerge in a simple youth to become a real man in the world. John looked toward the building where he had had his office and where the players had dressed before each game.

John wondered where the man was who had written him to visit this place one more time. He was intrigued by the man's letter, which was simple and to the point. The man had requested his presence on this date of Dec 7. This letter had informed him that he would receive an item, which would be most precious to him, and he would cherish it every day of his life. John could not understand the momentous importance of this date. All he could remember was that he had spent one year of his life here at this Ivy League prep school. Now, it had been taken over by a local church for the instruction of inner city kids who were bused in to attend a highly intensive instruction in science and mathematics. World War II had ended the sport of lacrosse for the duration of the war, and the sport had never really come back as far as he knew. He moved that spring to Canada to teach Chemistry in Montreal and coached track and field on the side to earn a little extra money. The following summer, he found a coaching position at Ashland College where he stayed until a year ago when he retired. He cherished the fall and the spring on the Ashland campus. It was a beautiful region with the rolling hills and numerous trees and flower gardens. There was something poetic about the leaves falling off the trees, the disappearance of the greenery in the fall on the campus and the rebirth of the flowers and the trees forming their leaves again in the spring. There were times during these two seasons he would just walk the campus to feel the change that was occurring.

The wet, cold weather was starting to penetrate his heavy brown coat. He had heard on the radio that there was a high probability of snow flurries. He turned and started to move toward the car when he heard a cry in the distance.

"Sir!" There was a short pause from the voice he heard in the distance. John turned around and saw a short man moving quickly toward him.

"Please wait!" came another cry from the man.

"I'm so glad you came. I wasn't sure what time I told you to be here." The young man's voice said in a softer voice.

"I've just come from practice." The man said trying to grasp a breath between each word. John stood motionless. He could not understand what this young person wanted from him or what he could give that he would cherish. John could see that the face of the person he was speaking to have been brutally hit on more than one occasion. The boy's nose had obviously been broken, possibly several times. There was a long scar just above his left eyebrow, and a longer scar on the boy's right lower jaw. John thought fast about what kind of practice this young man was talking about. Perhaps, he had been playing ice hockey for one of the local schools around here. John remembered the Harvard prep school down the road about a mile. The school was still running at full blast. Money does that. John had seen this at Ashland.
The young boy just stood there in front of him. John was still trying to gain his composure. John looked at this boy. He was barely over five foot tall. His body was stocky. From the look of his thick muscled neck, John could assume the boy's body was solid and had no fat. The thought entered his mind that this kid could be a varsity lineman for one of the prep school football teams in the area. Still examining this youth, John suddenly became irritated. Why had he come over two hundred miles to this strange place, where he had not been for over four decades. Granted, his time was abundant since his retirement, but this was his time and especially his money he had spent on gas for the trip.

"I've got to go now! I'm getting cold! It's starting to snow." John spoke rudely directly leaning into the boy's face.

"Hey! Wait! Please!" The boy pleaded. John could see the boy's large brown eyes. They seemed to beg for him to stay. This did not change John's mindset. He was tired from the journey in his old car, and he could start to feel the cold wind penetrate his old wool coat. He would probably catch his death of cold and have to spend money on a doctor's visit if he came down with one. On his limited income, he didn't need this or the aggravation that this young boy was giving him.

"I know you don't know me!" The youth exclaimed while John turned and started to walk away from this meeting.

"You knew my father!" The boy exclaimed louder. John stopped and wondered who his father could have been. He had been caught off guard. He was cold, tired, frustrated, and now hungry. He should have stopped at one of the fast food places along the road. It was too late now to do anything about his growling stomach.

John immediately took four steps forward. This placed him inches away and squarely in front of the stocky youth. John looked at the boy.
Both individuals were motionless and speechless. The boy looked directly into John's face. John looked at this boy who had aroused his curiosity and wondered what connection he had with him.

Who in the hell could he be a descendant of? He had never coached football. This was the only connection this boy could have with him. John thought to himself while he silently examined the person in front of him. He had seen thousands of faces and bodies like this during his coaching career. Anyone could have been this boy's father. The only players with scars were the lacrosse players he had coached here years ago. After the first month of play, they seemed to be immersed in the game. The only purpose in their existence was to play this crazy torturous game. Not injury, the length of the game nor the intensity mattered to these young players.

John noticed the boy was slowly moving his right hand from the heavy coat he was wearing. John took a step back. A range of thoughts ran through his mind. Did the kid have a weapon? What was going to happen next?
John fixed his eyes on the boy's right side while he took another step back. He had not expected these events.

The boy's hand emerged from his pocket with his right palm open flat. John could see he held a colored necklace. Intrigued, he took a step forward. John could see the necklace better now. The necklace was woven with crudely shaped alternating black and red beads.

Instantly, he recognized and remembered the time, the place and whom he had given the crude Indian necklace to. He had personally made each necklace from some beads he had bought at an art shop in a nearby town. He had made these necklaces for his lacrosse team that had played on this field where he and this boy now stood. John had never seen such an odd ball group of boys wanting to play the game of lacrosse. All were seniors except one. They were so awkward, thin, and out of shape. The boy interrupted his thoughts.

"You gave this to my father years ago. He gave it to me last year just before he died. He asked me to give it to you." The boy spoke boldly.

"He told me the story that you told the team. He said you told the team at least once a week when I visited him at the nursing home. He wore the necklace all the time." The boy stopped speaking.

John looked directly into the boy's eyes. He could see his eyes begin to water. Doing this was important to this boy. John stood motionless in front him. He knew this was the boy's duty to his father and had to be accomplished.

"He was the tenth man on your team. He told me, you only used him when you had no choice." The boy stopped speaking again and bowed his head indicating he was ashamed that his father had been only a substitute player. Raising his head, the boy started to speak again. "He was built like me - short and stocky. But he was heavier than I am. You probably would called him a "fat boy" back then. I'm all muscle." There was another pause from the boy standing in front of him. John could see the pride being re-established in the boy's face and his whole posture change when he spoke his last sentence.

John stared in amazement at this youth. He was speechless.

"I'm like him. I play Baggataway. The other players I play with make fun of me, when I tell them the story, you would tell the players and my father; of how the medicine man would take the young warriors down to the river to hold the ritual before the game of Baggataway with a neighboring tribe. This was one way a young man could prove himself as a man and a proud warrior of their tribe. I told them an Iroquois warrior would play Baggataway for days on end. The field of play could be over several acres of forest, not a field of 110 yards by 60 yards.

A ball was made of deerskin and a heavy stick made of a sturdy maple or oak limb with a narrow fork at the end of the stick. The cup was covered with strands of hardened deerskin to catch the ball. There was no formed cup to rest the ball like we use today. The warrior wore only his loincloth. He had no protective gear to protect his body from the blows of his opponents." The boy paused breathing deeply, reliving the intense tension his mind and body possessed. John still stood in silence. He was astonished at the boy's approach to the game. He had the same emotion as the boys he had once instructed.

"My father wanted me to give you this." The boy said. Both of their eyes looked at the strand of beads.

"He told me that you told the tale of the medicine man taking the tribe's team before each game. To tell you the truth, everyone, even my father thought you had lost your mind. But after the third time, nearly everyone realized this was not an American game. The French had taken the game from the American Indians, and some forgotten missionary put the label of lacrosse on the game. This was a warrior's game to establish dominance over another tribe. Baggattaway was a game for the chosen few who could endure and rise to the cause of the team and not of individual desires. This game taught pride in one's actions on or off the playing field. Only the true leader could withstand and rise above whatever he faced in his world." The boy stopped speaking, and each looked into each other's eyes. John finally remembered the change in the individuals on his team. They had changed mentally, physically and developed a fire of desire in their spirit to perform beyond their physical capabilities. Before him, he saw the same fire he had created in those youth's years ago.

"He told me about the match that was held on this day some forty years ago. You took the team down to the creek the evening at dusk before the last game. Over there." The boy paused, pointing with his clutched fist over to the right. In the far distance, they could both see where the little creek still flowed. They first thought it a little crazy when you dressed up in only a piece of loin skin around your waist. You told them the story, but you had a green and black necklace that you threw on the creek's rocks shattering the strand of beads with the bottom of your bare foot. You claimed this was a sign that the team would crush their foe in the coming match. The team understood later the match that they would play next was not just another match. This was a spiritual and personal issue for each player to deal with themselves and as a team as a whole. Win or Lose. This game would affect them the rest of their lives.

You and the Harvard prep team thought your team members were crazy when they saw the players with their painted faces. My father told me that the team got together and decided to decorate their faces and arms like Huron Indians going to war. They figured that this might give them a slight advantage in the first quarter.
Remember, they yelled and screamed like idiots. At least this is what my father told me." A smile appeared on John's face. He could see and hear his players that day.

"It worked. We outscored them two to one the first quarter. They came back and by the second quarter, the score was tied. In the second half, each team developed a desire to win at any cost. Players started to get hurt. There were only bruises. As the game went on the intensity increased, several players lost teeth and blood began to appear on every player.

My father claims, it was his team's stubbornness not to accept defeat at the hands of their opponent. Pride has its place; he would always tell me.

Just before the end of the fourth quarter. Jerome, our goalie, was hit on the right forearm. The break was clean and another person had to take his place. The only person left was my father. The 'fat boy'.

The Harvard prep team had at least ten more people to give their players a break, but we had only my father to relieve his teammates."

The game ended in a tie. 8 to 8.

At the end, something strange happen.   The players would not leave the field. Each team wanted a decisive victory. Suddenly, my father screamed a loud war cry followed by the words "Victory!" "Let's play Baggataway." The rest of his teammates followed his chant. The Harvard team started to yell. "Let's Play!" You and the other coach talked and decided to let the teams play until there was a Victor." The young boy was quiet.   John looked at this individual standing in front of him.   There were no words he could say. The boy had said everything. John could not tell how many minutes had passed before the boy spoke again. From the tone of his voice, John could tell the boy was nearly finished.

"I wish that I could say that my father won, but they lost.   Only by a goal, and only five goals were scored.   Three for the other team and two for my father's team. They played for two more hours.   More blood was spilled, and more teeth were lost. My father's team left their mark on each member of the opposite team.   My father swore no injury was inflicted on purpose but only in combat to score, to protect or secure the ball."

When I was young, I would sit after dinner on Sunday and listen to him tell of his exploits in the military and his life. I guess you are wondering why I am so young. I'm eighteen.   I go to Harvard in the fall to study medicine.   My father finally married after Korea.   After he had died, I went through his personal effects.   I never saw so many medals.

Funny, he hated war - Especially the killing.   After he had married my mother, he started a small business to keep himself busy I think, to teach me about the business world.   He would comment later on how he wished that I did not have to go to war and experience the Hell of killing another person.

After he had opened the business, I was amazed at how people respected him, and I guess feared him. He learned that from you that season.
"This was the way to live life. One must give everything to what you do no matter what the task; one must overcome the obstacles life puts in front of you. There must be Honor; Duty and one must go beyond what you think you can do. I'm the only one to care about my grades or about my future on my team.   The other guys, they like to drink and party. I know if I am to meet the task I must approach everything like the game of Baggattaway." The boy stopped speaking. Both men stood facing each other.   John knew now the individual was not a boy but a man among men even at his young age.
The young man broke the silence again.

"I am sorry. I have kept you too long in this cold weather. Here is the necklace.   He wanted you to have it," the young man said, lifting his hand upward extending his open palm with the exposed Indian necklace toward John.

"I can't take it," John replied.

"Yes. You can." The young man said.

"No. It's yours, and the necklace is in your blood and life. You must keep it. I'm old, and I'll die within a couple of years." John said, motioning a refusal by pushing the young man's palm closed.

"No." The young man said sternly.

"Why?" Asked John.

"Before he died my father told me that I would find seven more necklaces in his safe-deposit box. Most came from the Pacific in the war.

I expect that I will get the rest when they died. They all kept track of each other. My father was the goalie. They all looked up to him after the match that day.

They figured that the "fat boy" would lose the game for them in the last quarter of regulation time. He didn't. He became a leader then.

After he had finished telling me the tale one-day of that day when he was in the nursing home, he told me how he lost the game. Three of them ganged up on him. Two of the opponents ran full force into him sandwiching his body between their two bodies making him unable to move while the third opponent tossed the ball toward the goal. He would make the final comment to me. "That's life. You do the best that you can and a little more."

A year ago I met the forward on his team. He told me why my father missed blocking the ball by inches.

"No. This is yours." The young man said, emphatically giving the necklace to John.

"All I can say is "Thanks." No words or trophy can replace this necklace." John replied.

"I am the one to give you the thanks. You have given my father and me the experience of the Baggataway.

Without speaking, both individuals turned around in opposite directions.

John quickly cranked his old Ford station wagon, turning on the heater. His body was cold but not his soul. He stayed there in the station wagon looking at the deserted playing field watching the snow gently fall.

I'm Different

"Hey!" a voice rang out making Pat look up. There stood a young man about six feet tall. His body structure was sinewy and muscular with no body fat.

"Harry," the young man paused and looked around.

"He told me that I probably need to come to talk to you....and you'd under-stand," he said as Pat motioned with his right arm to sit down the adjacent bam-boo chair.

"You want something to drink.....it's really hot this summer," Pat asked.

"This is cool from where I've been," the man interjected pausing after he spoke. "I've been over there twice in three years," he followed. Pat understood where he had been - either in South East Asia or the Far East."

There was eerie silence between the two men.

Pat was waiting for him to speak again. He was the one that had come to tell him something. Pat examined the young man's face. It had a hollow expression with his face showing his cheek bones. Pat looked into his deep blue eyes. His pupils were roaming the exterior of the room. They had the depth to them where Pat couldn't see the bottom of this persons' soul or where his foundation was based. Pat surmised he had seen action that only a very few had seen in the battle between the rational world and the radical extremist.

"My name is Michael," the young man voice broke the dead silence.

"I've been twice," the dead silence appeared again.

"The first time, I came back, I noticed the difference between me and my sur-roundings and the people that I grew up with.....This first six months over there, I jumped at any noise, and when the loud ones came, I wanted to run under any-thing that was around, a truck or anything that I could get under.....but I noticed all the new comers after I had been there four months did this.

It was just normal behavior." Pat noticed Michael hadn't move a muscle in his body. He had both of his feet flat on the oak wood floor and with both legs parallel to each other. His upper body sat at a nine-degree angle to the bottom of the bamboo chair. Both of his arms were at a right angle to his side with his open palms flat on his blue jeans. The only motion was his lips and the pupils of s that were shifting when he wasn't speaking to Pat. When he spoke, he looked directly at Pat in a trance state.

I was standing watch about three months into my tour. I was watching the woman who looked three months pregnant slowly walking toward our post. The bomb went off prematurely. After the blast, I was cover with her blood, and I had been hit by parts of her body. I stood in the hot shower for a long time wanting to wash off the blood off me.   During the next couple of nights, I had to get up and take showers before I got over that feeling of being covered in her blood.

I asked myself, " This Is HELL!"

It was in the hundreds until the night fell and then it was cold with a wind coming from the East," Michael stopped speaking.   Pat held his tongue.   This was Michael's forum, not his and he wanted to tell someone whatever was in side him.   He had seen this young man a couple of days ago talking to Harry while he bought a girlie magazine and some cigarettes.   He had spent a good time , while at the counter talking to Harry.

"I was alone!" Michael's voice broke the silence.

"I just got my mom and a sister....my father died last year.

After the bomb incident, everyone came with support and tried to pick up my spirits...."Pat noticed Michael shake his head in a negative manner....It took me four days not to be suspicious of anyone that didn't wear a uniform....but I always looked at any civilian that wasn't an American twice over....I was suspicious of anyone.

We - the guys - didn't care what color or what age you were as long you were dressed in an American uniform.....you were one of us and we or I didn't have to be afraid."

One time on patrol, we had to shoot a kid - heck he must have been only twelve years old - but he had been firing at us for an hour before Jeff got him with a lucky shot.   When we got behind the window opening where he had been firing, we were amazed that it was just a kid handling the automatic weapon.   We all shook our heads at what we had found. ....we didn't have a choice.   It was either him or us, and you know what comes first when you get shot at.

It's him, and you hope like hell you don't get it.   Granted, the medic is there or somewhere near you to get patch up and to get the helicopter and get out you within ten minutes.   But if you get hit, you'll never be the same.   I don't care what they say.

I think it makes you 'nuts.' … nuts in the sense you're scared to death you'll die, and a part of you won't be there after the 'horse doctors' get hold of you." Michael stopped talking.   He turned his head left, then right and did this again.

'You know some of those guys came back after a month in the hospital, and they could have gone home and never come back.....but they loved the hunt for the bad guys.   It scared me to sneak around a building waiting to find someone that wanted to kill you.

I had too many bullets come within inches of me," Michael was quiet again and looked Pat directly.

"You know its no fun to really know there is this person out there who isn't playing and really wants to kill you." Michael was quiet. Pat nodded in agreement.

"You form friends with people that you never thought you would let sleep on your stomach while you were sleeping." Pat noticed a slight smile on his lips.

"There was this guy from South Chicago. He was black - black as black can get. His name was Jake. Being from the South over the years I have let those folks be and do what they have a right to do. Now, my great great grandfather fought in the Civil War, and his son was the Great Grand Wizard of that unspeakable organization.

It was two months before I was to come home. Jake was pouring diesel fuel on the grass on the banks of the river bank. We did this because the rebels would come up the river at night and they would shoot off hand grenades into our camp. There was a loud blast. I was back at the truck. The grass started to burn. I yelled for Jake.

He didn't answer.

It took nearly an hour before we could look for Jake.
Well, we found pieces of him, and I put them into a body bag. I could have just sat down and cried like a baby, but I was a man and solider. Soldiers don't cry when they have a job to do!

I cried all night that night.

When I came back, I went and lived at home. I started to take a college course at the college near the lake.

During class, I looked around. I was the oldest there. At first, I thought this was what was the matter but after two weeks, I knew it was something else. They were young girls who were always cuddled together laughing or giggling about some cute little boy one was dating....I couldn't help but overhear their conversations because they were so loud.

Half way through the semester, I noticed half of the people in the class had stopped coming and after mid-term another quarter had left the class. I had an A in the class, and the professor came to me telling me, I didn't need to finals because of work and the grades, I had in the course. The next quarter I took five classes and held a solid B average for all courses. The third quarter I only took two courses and went fishing the rest of the time. Half way through the semester, I got a letter telling in July that I would be going again.

When I hit the ground, I knew how to react.
I still reacted again to sounds of the bombing. Heck, it took me four months to adjust to cars' backfiring when I got back home the first time but this time nothing bothered me.

I stood my guard duty, and I was luckily, this time, nothing happen." Michael stopped talking.

When I went on patrol the first time - Pat noticed Michael's eyes sprang open like this was the time take in every element that surrounded this young man.

I was a little anxious and that feeling my number would be coming up when I arrived. When jumped off the jeep on to the dusty bare ground, I pulled my rifle into position it was like riding a bike after ten years not being on one. I could feel the adrenaline flowing through my veins. I was apart of the pack again. We were like the 'three musketeers' 'one for all - one for each other. Nothing happen that day, but I couldn't sleep that night. I was scared to death, but I liked it. I had missed it while I was back home but I still didn't want to be there. I thought of the 'duty' I had obligated myself for and the education that this hellish tour would be paying for when I got back on American soil.

A strange thing happen in that year, I never got close to anyone. A couple of guys in our group 'bought the farm' as the saying goes and it didn't bother me and
I didn't shed one tear." There was an eerie silence.

"I guess, the episode with 'Jake' had conditioned me not to get close to any-one. I noticed this in the past year when I was home for the first time. I didn't get close to anyone. I was aloof with my mother and with anyone who I would have contact with. I spent a lot of time either fishing or in the library reading. I took a couple of women out, but they seem so childish and stuck-up wanting me to buy them this or that, to make them happy.

Well, in the morning when the squad would gather, I would look forward to the hunt. It was a cat and mouse game for me....and I was the cat. On the average, our squad would pull in five to ten suspected terrorist in a week.

Then....it happen!" Pat's s pop open wide. What did this innocent looking kid do? Pat thought.

It was really hot that day. I bet it was 120 degrees in the shade. It was two in the afternoon. We walking down this alley. A bomb went off in the street behind us.
There were four of us....and armed with an automatic rifle. plus the other stuff. We turned around. We saw this crowd of people carrying a rocket launcher and weapons. We all cried out, "Stop!! Stop!!!" We saw them point their weapons toward us. Our squad leader yelled, "Take cover." The shooting started. I got behind this car that had four flat tires and no windows in it. I started firing in the direction of the on coming assault. After fifteen minutes I had emptied both of rifles. There was a dead quietness after we had stop firing. None of our group had been hit." Michael was quite, and he looked down at the oak floor in front of him.

"We walked slowly toward the group bodies on the ground. I had my pistol out and the safety off.

It was a bloody mess.

The five of us just stood there the middle of the bodies; we had just shot full of our bullets.   I first noticed the three men who had been in front carrying the weapons but behind them were four women and five children.

In killing the three men, our bullets had gone straight through them and killed the women, or after the men had fallen, we killed the women and the children." Michael raised his head and looked at Pat directly in the s.

"They didn't have any weapons," Michael said in clear, pragmatic tone of voice.

"I just stood there looking at those women and children lying on the ground. They were all bloody.   I hadn't bargained for this but this a part of the war. The squad leader yelled out, "Frank call the Officer of the Day on the phone. Tell him that we have civilian fatalities."   I think, I remember him coming to each of us telling us, "Hey, they were just in the way.   It's not our fault they were at the wrong place.   There were probably their wives and children."

Each of us was taken into separate tents when we got back to camp. All our stories were the same, so they just told us 'let it be.'

The next week, they flew me out for some reason to Germany where I had to tell my story about ten times to five different people.   The last person to talk to me was a two-star general. He just told me, "Go home and forget it and go back to school." Michael looked around.

"That's easier said than done. I killed innocent people, granted they were at the wrong place, but still they were women and little children." Michael stopped talking.   He looked up at the large old clock above the old red cooler.

"I've got to go," he said quickly.

"You know after I got home two weeks ago everything was different. This town is so small, and the people just walk about like it is nothing to have 'peace'.
The first night in my bed, I couldn't get to sleep.   I laid there at first I thought about my father and my mother. I thought about the first girl that I made love too. They all seemed so distant and far away.   I was alone - all alone. I was different from the first time I had come back home.

Now, I was even more 'different'," he was quiet again.

I know now why my father was so distant at times. … oh, I didn't tell you, he was Vietnam Vet.   He died of that agent orange stuff; they put out in Nam.

"I've got to go. I've got a phone call to make to the University if I am to go in a couple of weeks.

"Thanks' for letting me tell you this.   I wonder if you understand what has hap- pened to me." Michael pushed down with both palms on his knees as he straighten himself out the bamboo chair.   Pat did the same out of respect for the story this man had just told him and was about to speak when Michael spoke again.

"You know. I know, I will be different for the rest of my life. I have to find some kind of 'peace' within myself......what's funny...remember Jake. Well, we were talking about that one night until day break. What is crazy or not so crazy - each of us has to find that 'peace within ourselves and no pill, dope, woman or booze will find it for us." Michael paused and looked around and toward the front of the Smoke House like he was looking for something.

"What's really strange that was the night before Jake 'bought the farm," he said shaking his head in a negative manner.

"You have to go make that phone call. I do appreciate you telling me your story." Pat said placing his right hand out for Michael to shake it.

"Yes, you are different but you've survived," Pat said as Michael put forth his left hand and grip Pat's like a vise and Pat did the same.

Michael turned and left.

As Pat sat down, he could hear the cowbell clang as the young man left. Pat thought of the journey this young man had taken and hoped he would find the 'peace' he would be searching for.

Pat knew this young man would be 'different' for the rest of his life.

But, this is just a part of War.

The Home Town Hero

I gazed at the water.

I was mesmerized my the invisible wind making the surface of the water moving toward me.

I thought of him.   He was the same now as the wind.

I look up and to my left I saw the old truck park next to a tree where I had parked. I smiled.   We had restored the old 66 chevy long bed truck together during the summer before his senior year where he could drive it back and forth from high school and from his part-time job at the grocery store.   With the metallic Fire Engine red glossy paint job that his friend's father had put on the truck, he probably thought h was driving in the best style any teenager could drive beside a GTO convertible.

We were close. At least I thought we were. I was wrong in a sense for I let him grow up and stand on his on feet. The incident that prove me wrong and right at the same time was his decision to go - to volunteer and to put aside his dreams of being a professional baseball player and putting off his last two years of college - to go to war.

I could feel gentle wind meeting my face. The wind had a cold bite to it. The time of year was when the northern winds were coming down South to met the air stream coming from the Gulf.

I still didn't"t understand why he had to go, but he was like me during the Vietnam War or Conflict has the historians call it.   I had to volunteer when my friends went to Canada. Granted, I had since debated if I had done the right thing but I would come to the same conclusion that I would have done the same. He had come to the same conclusion.

I looked at the water again. The water was clam, and the wind had dissipated into thin air just like he had disappeared from my life and his mother's life.   This was not to say of the young woman he had introduced us to only months before he had told me of his decision.

I had been yelling at him because I knew of the dangerous and the fate of young men that go to war. I had told him to let the other young men go and get killed. He was deadly quiet during my lecturing and yelling about the evils and futility of war. Suddenly, he spoke in a soft voice after I had asked many times, "Why? Why?"

"It's my duty. It"s about my country and it's about what is right in the world. Not just around here," He replied.

I was speechless for I knew down deep this was the same answer that I come up when I sat in a foxhole soaking wet, bullets passing me by and carrying my dead comrade's bodies where they could be sent back to their love ones.

I heard to my left the leaves brushings against each other as the Northern wind pick up through the branches of dead leaves on the limbs of the trees near the water.

I knew where his answer had come from. His answers came from the years of taking him to church and teaching him the lessons from right from wrong. He had gained the knowledge of duty from being a Boy Scout. I smiled.

I remembered of him helping a neighbor when the neighbor was despair need of someone to do his chores around his place while he was sick. He had done this without anyone directing him. I wouldn't or anyone would have known of what he was doing if it wasn't for him being late one evening in coming home. He had told his mother
matter of fact when she had asked why he was coming home so late after work. His mother just told him that was nice of him. He just said nothing in return.

I could not believe of the people in town who came forward to tell me of the stories of what he had done for them without any pay after it was reported in the newspaper that he was killed in action,

I look toward the water again.

Then, there were the people that came also to scorn the futility of his death that his young life had been wasted in vain for political purposes and for the re-sources of this country. I was amazed at the bitterness that encompassed these individuals.
I bent down and pick up a pebble.

I had knew his commanding officer before they left and asked him to send me monthly reports on him. This was not to say to keep him safe for me and especially his mother who had cried at night for months after he left.

He had done his best.

I was amazed of the reports his commander had written me about him. He told me how he had time and time put his life in peril to make sure his comrades would not come into harms way and why he had met the fate that he finally met.
I was surprised at the medals that he was recommended to receive and the final Purple Heart that he was given in the end for saving numerous of lives of civilians.

I lean forward has I rose up throwing the pebble and making it skip across the water.

He was like the pebble. He had danced. He had done, what he had thought was correct and right. He had given his best and his life for what he believed in.
What else is there in this world? He was like the pebble at the bottom the lake. He would be a part of the lives he had to prevent from injury or death and given the world a chance to be a
better place to live in.

"What other great purpose can a person have in this life," I said in a soft voice to myself as I stood erect and looked that the old Chevy truck.
'Time was to go and console his mother and his grieving girl friend.' I thought to myself, - for I had finally come to terms of my son's life and him dying in the fashion that he did."

THE WALL

Al held an unlit cigarette while standing beneath a medium size oak tree. A couple of yards in front of him the Wall stood. He had mixed feelings of why he had come to this place, but he knew that he had to be here at this particular time.

He moved slowly toward the walkway where the black marble monument began to emerge from the manicured green lawn. Al could see the glistening effect of the sun on the raindrops left on the shiny black marble.

The young Korean woman had captured the essence of the dignity of the names the memorial bore in the cold marble which had fallen during the conflict his country had been involved in for over ten years. This conflict had created a chasm that would never heal. The arising intersecting slabs of cold black, blue marble symbolized the rising of the dead of the thousands of Americans' who had followed their leaders into a futile war. This wasn't a conflict or a police action but a political war. A political war fought in the jungles, where the fighting was unlike anything a human had ever experienced before.

Along the declining walkway toward the intersecting black slabs on both sides, Al could see numerous individuals kneeling and praying, feeling the etched marble with their fingers. Others were standing in a somber state focusing on nothing but probably a memory of the person or the last place they had been with this person.

There was an emptiness inside Al, while he looked at these people who walked by or stood along the Wall. His stomach was tight. Instinctively, he wanted to leave. He knew, he couldn't.

Why did I have to come to this place? Was it closure or to acknowledge of what these men who were posted on the Wall did for him and gave him in that year? Some he had only known casually and only for a couple of days. The only thing he knew was that he had experienced the reality of what he had experienced in Vietnam as these men had.

Al stopped suddenly. The hot sun was bearing down on his body. His forehead was sweating. Al felt the perspiration dripping underneath his armpits and the wetness' on his broad back. He remembered sweating like this his first day in

Vietnam. The place was the Danang Air Force Base. The date was August 18, 1973. The place was chaos. Everyone seemed to be going in every direction. The heat was unbearable, and this was compounded more by the humidity factor. He had heard it stayed this hot nearly year round, and the humidity was a fact of life in this part of the world. He was amazed that there were no accidents or anyone killed at this insane pace. He learned this was false; at least two were killed each day because of someone's carelessness in Vietnam.

Al didn't know as he stepped off the C-10 transport plane, he would be changed for the rest of his life. He had been told that he had an office job after he had graduated top of his class at Radio School. He had been led into a false promise. The second day he found himself on a chopper to some God-forsaken base camp for six months before he went to R & R in Singapore. Singapore had the women and the drugs that allowed a man to escape the hell; he had endured those months. The women could send a man by their little tricks; they had been taught by their madam.

He placed the unfiltered cigarette in the corner of his mouth underneath the bushy mustache. Al had had this since his second week a base camp. The guys had made fun of his attempting to grow hair underneath his nose. He wondered if it was the drugs, the beer, the women, or facing the uncertain death that had changed him. This was not to mention being shot at from Charlie from the bush, just being plain scared to hell that he would not live the day out. Whatever it was, it was made his body develop into a solid lean masculine structure.

Out of his platoon in the first two months, over half of its members were either sent home in a body bag or wounded seriously enough to be sent to Hawaii. Those guys were the lucky ones; the ones were alive, he always thought. Down deep, he knew they would be the most messed up when they returned to the States. Granted they would get a check every month, but everyone in the States hated them because either they didn't like the war or did not want to be associated with the results of the abyss inside America. Al's eyes were focused on the wooden matchbox he had pulled from his right front pocket.

While he lighted the cigarette, a smile formed on his lips and face. This was where he had first smoked a joint. Drugs were his preference to the beer, which flowed like water. Marijuana was used to escape quickly the horrors that that was seen – done that day and the day before or to face another day and night that exist for him. This was a war, not a conflict or an assistance program to prevent communism from spreading. Al now understood his father's actions when he had asked about Korea when he was a child. His father would always change the subject or leave the room if he was confronted with the conversation about war. Al took a deep drag of the burning tobacco.

The fighting in Nam was like an office job. At an appointed time, his squad would leave the base camp and in a couple of hours to a couple of days they would be picked up by a couple of choppers. If someone were killed or wounded in the field, a chopper would pick them up after the action. He could remember at the base camp when they were waiting for orders to go into the bush, a chopper would ferry pizzas in Danang or Saigon. On numerous occasions, the helicopter would bring in stewardesses from one of the contract air-transports to camp. Each one had probably earned a couple of thousand doing her tricks. Al figured they gave the pilot a share of their earnings.

Al released the smoke he had accumulated in his lungs. The white smoke rose up hiding his face. His smile disappeared. He could still hear the wrapping of the chopper blades at night sometimes if the circumstances were right. For the most part, he had adjusted to the killing and hell he had experienced. He could still see at times the two kids, a boy of around ten and a young teenage girl; he had killed. There was no choice. It was either them or him. One had a hand grenade, and the other had a Russian AK- 47. He had heard other stories of whole villages being wiped out; women, children and old people that were killed because the villages were one of Charlie's bases of operations. Al lowered the smoking cigarette beside his side. He had also heard the stories of the senseless random killing of innocent civilians because some of psyched up Lt. was on a rampage to get a higher body account.

He dropped the burning cigarette on the green grass and crushed the smoldering tobacco with the bottom of his right shoe. After the first week, he had gotten his first kill. Al was ordered to check one of those tunnels where Charlie had stored his rice, guns, and ammunition. Al learned later that this was part of the Ho Chi Mi Trail. He had been chosen to go down into the tunnel because he was smallest and newest member of the squad. The tunnel was infested with snakes, rats, and the walls were dripping a wet some slimy substance. He had killed his first person on this journey. He killed was barely sixteen and probably scared to death just like himself, when they faced each other. He had been lucky that day. Both had let out numerous rounds from each of their automatic guns at each other. After the squad had blown-up the chase of ammunition, a chopper came, and they went back to base camp. The squad was given six cases of beer that night. Al drank his share but threw-up all that night. He could still see the young mans' eyes when he closed his eyes that night.

He was cheered as the hero of the day. This act had brought him into the fold of the squad. Now, he was one of them. The next day as he was nursing his hangover, waiting for the squad's next assignment, he looked and examined each member of his squad. They were just like him young and mostly misfits that had been drafted just like him, but they were now seasoned veterans by the killing and the surviving of this day.

Living; day by day in combat in the jungle, classified you as a veteran or just being a plain survivor in this hot, humid hellhole.

A smile formed on Al's face again. Before Vietnam, he couldn't stand Mo-town music, but Lee from Detroit had changed that. He kind of understood, of the sort, the meaning of this kind of music had for these people. But Lee was dead; he had thrown himself on a grenade the VC had thrown into a foxhole with two other people in it, and they were white. A man did strange things for the man next you.

A grin formed slightly on Al's lips while he pulled a pack of open cigarettes out of his front pocket. They had all been strangers thrown together from all parts of the country. Each individual was counting the days to leave base camp for either their flight home or R & R at some government retreat. Pulling the single cig-arette out of the pack, Al laughed softly. They had all formed a bond between each other. Each bond was different. There was a bond even with the "lifers" as they called them. Most of the lifers were on their second or third tour. They en-joyed the killing and could not wait to go out to hunt Charlie. A person could see it in their eyes. Living on the edge between life and death was their soul purpose in life. There was one unwritten bond between the men Al had fought with. The common bond was survival and knowing each person had to go beyond himself to save himself and the man next to him.

He lighted the cigarette and started to walk on the walkway next the Wall to the intersection of the two pieces of black, blue marble. His soul and mind felt a longing to see the men that he knew who were listed on this wall.

He could not believe the day; he had received his orders to catch the chopper back to Saigon. On the flight back to Saigon, he thought of how he had changed. He had gained over fifty pounds; most of the guys had lost weight. Al was different. He spent most of his time in base camp lifting weights with Lee and a Polish fellow named Ski. Al had turned himself into a muscle-bound hu-man specimen. He knew that his mind would never be the same with all the killing, the drugs, and the realization of the lies the government was telling about the war.

He understood now what happen to people in war.

Al stood motionless in front of the marble slab. At least the government had not screwed-up this tribute to his fellow comrades. Each name was listed by the year, month, and date the person had died. He thought taking the cigarette out of his mouth.

December 29

HARRY F. STEPSON
FRED J. WATKINS
JOSEPH JONES

The list ran on at least twenty more.   Here was Jones' name in the marble. Al put his fingers on the etched name.   He had taken a bullet meant for Ski. Both of them were in a foxhole together in the outer perimeter.   Joe had taken his place behind the 90mm. Ski had turned to get a drink of water.   Joe fell over dead with a single bullet in the head. Joe was going back for Christmas and going to get married to his high school sweet heart on the 31st of December.   He was going to work as a bookkeeper for his father while he went to college to become an accountant. He always talked about making it big when he got his CPA. Al could feel the dampness coming from his eyes. Ski had suddenly disappeared into the bush after Joe had got it. We could hear Ski firing his M-16 and people screaming when they had been hit. The guys in the squad stayed away from Ski for a month after this incident - he knew what the 'kill' was all about now.

It had been Skip that had come to him after this incident. There was a strange bond with him and AL. Skip was strange anyway.   The last Al had heard about Skip was that he had gone back to Nam one more time and had gotten wounded. He either be retired by now or would be getting a check for some reason from the Army.   After, Al had heard that he had moved to a remote island off the coast of Georgia. He was living the life of a semi-hermit.   He would only go into town for his monthly check, and would catch wild pigs for the tourists to eat, using only a 12" knife to catch and kill the wild pig.

Al flicked the burning cigarette on the grass in front of the Wall.   He was still a mess inside.   After he had returned to the States, he worked construction with his father and married Julie.   Things weren't the same with her.   He had taken her virginity away a week before he left for Nam.   Sex, after Nam was different.

26

Al's outlook was different about everything. Julie left him after a couple of drunken weekends. Life had become meaningless and really not worth living especially at night when nightmares would come back. A month ago he figured to end it all with an overdose of sleeping pills the doctor had prescribed. He had bought the pills and was going to do the deed when he received a phone call from Joe's father. In the phone call Joe's father had told him that after six years, he had finally gone through Joe's personal papers. He apologized for the time delay, but Al knew about the denial that Joe's father was going through. Al had been in denial since the first day he had stepped into base camp and realized this place was going to be worse than hell itself.

A grin appeared on Al's lips. His fingers were still touching the etched name of Joe. Al would always remember what Joe's father had told him that day. Joe had written his father telling him about how Joe appreciate Al going beyond the orders the squad leader had given; placing himself always in front of danger and placing him out of danger, that is, going first into the tunnels and finding Charlie. Everyone hated this job, but this was now Al's task on every patrol if a tunnel was found.

Al turned around and saw the setting sun. One more day was finished. He had lived another day. The night would probably be rough, but he would live throughout the long night. There had to be a reason for him to be living. Al thought wiping the moistness from both his cheeks.

In turning, he thought about going to college. He could meet some women his age at night school. I could earn more money and maybe find another career.

Al turned around so he could look squarely at the Wall again.

Sitting in the old 75 FORD, Al paused one more time before he cranked the truck.

He wondered why he had survived, and those died.

The Vigil

I walked slowly toward the advancing waves letting my bare feet to be barely covered by the cool salt water. The water seemed to tease the waves to just touch the hem of my full flowing dress and then pull away. The night ocean water was cold, and the coldness made me feel alive.

Backing off to where the sand was still wet from the outgoing tide, I had walked, letting the wet sand go between my toes. The sand made my entire body feel the same as when we had walked together in the late evening during the latter years with him. He had brought out the best in me, as he did everything that he touched.

Glancing seaward, I wondered if he would ever return. My entire spirit and body wanted him back so much. However, deep inside, I knew, he would never return. Some nights I would arise around two or three in the morning with just my robe on, sit on the porch, and watch the rolling sea. I would look at the sea and the beach until dawn, waiting and thinking of him.

I felt so alive in the evening, walking on the beach by myself. The ocean wind was one of the secrets of this wonderful feeling. The on-coming sea breeze would blow my short brown hair behind me when I faced its powerful force. Only then, could someone see the strands of white hair that were forming?

I never forgot the times when we would play chicken with the on-coming waves. The dearest times were when he would pick me up suddenly and jump into a wave, soaking every inch of our bodies.

At first, this would make me furious at him, but I love to take a large soft bath towel and dry his masculine body. After both had dried each other, we would hold each other closely before I would fall to sleep in his arms with him stroking my soft hair with his large hands.

My bare body underneath my full cotton dress tingled from the cold ocean wind touching me. The coldness made small goose bumps on my bare skin. My body hadn't changed much over the years, even after having four children. My body was still shapely.

Now my body was a bit more fleshy but still with a firmness that most men like in a woman. I was still amused when older, middle-aged men made a play for my attention. But, there was only one man for me. I had not seen him for eleven years.

I could remember seeing him for the first time at friend's birthday party thirty-five years ago. He was wearing his dress white officer's uniform and only an LTJG. He had a look about him that separated him from the other officers there. I could tell that he had an aura of destiny about him. From the reaction of the other officers, I had sensed that they would follow this man no matter where he led or sent them. I could tell by observing him that he was not overbearing or high strung. He had the ability to stay in the background and still control the conversation that he part of.

What really attracted me to him was his eyes. They were a deep dark blue, similar to the water in a lagoon in the South Pacific Sea that we had seen once. His eyes had a mysterious, mystical, element, combined with an acceptance which I learned to marvel and respect in the following years. He could communicate quite well just by using his eyes. He had the power to communicate his ideas and thoughts to nearly anyone and bring them to an understanding of his goals with just his glance.

I found this out in the fourth year of our marriage. He was on the way to becoming the youngest Lt. Commander in the Navy. In doing so, he would be designated to command his own fighter squadron of Phantom Jets, which I accused him of being his love instead of his family. In being squadron commander of the Phantom Jets, he could be sent directly into combat in Vietnam. I didn't want this. I wanted him to be near and arranged an interview with a leading passenger carrier. With my father's connections, he was guaranteed a promising career. My heart's desire was for him to be near to home over 80% of the time instead of 20% of the time.

I told him my plans at dusk during our walk on the beach. I had never seen him so disturbed and upset. I had seen him get upset for me doing something that would cross him, but not like this. He stopped abruptly, turned, and looked directly into my eyes. "You don't take care of me like a child. I'm an adult. I have my career. I have people depending on me. They have entrusted me with other people's lives. My men look up to me for leadership, and to treat them with respect as men. I'll be back in a couple of days. Besides, you know where I'll be, you are where I'll be." He said these things emphatically, and so quickly my head was spinning around and around.

What had I done? I only wanted to be near and care for him. My mind was confused and went over and over our conversation. I stayed on the beach late that night. Luckily the three children were at his mother's for the weekend. "I knew where he would be." He wouldn't be in a bar or with another woman. He would go to the BOQ and about five in the morning he would rise up and be in the cockpit of a Phantom Jet by six. He would probably fly until late in the evening. With his charisma, he could do almost anything that he wanted to do. He had the leadership quality that the higher-ups were looking for to lead the young officers. I could not understand what I had done wrong.

The breeze gradually increased in force upon my fragile body. When he returned home after several days away, he seemed to have a more determined presence about him. Inside, I was frantic and didn't know what to do or say to him. I did not want to lose him, but not because of the financial resources. Instead, I was part of this man's spirit. I now realized that I could not control him or his destiny. There was a part of me that could not be separated from him. He was a part of my life, that part that kept me living for the next day.

The sea breeze suddenly gushed in a different direction and made my short fluffy hair almost stand straight up. I could remember that evening, the three children playing some child's game and making a lot of noise in the back room. He came directly to me and started talking calmly. "I leave in the morning for Danang. I will fly to the carrier from there and take command of my squadron. I have to tell you a few things that I have been thinking about over the past few days." He paused, and I saw him take a deep breath. "We have been married for nearly four years. I married you because I love you. I'm not a child. I know my shortcomings. If I need help, I'll ask you for it. Over the past couple of years, you have learned to take responsibility for the household. I can't worry about paying the light bill or any of the other small details," he said softly. Pausing, he took his open right hand, touched my left cheek and wiped a single tear that was ready to fall.

"I love you. We will always be with each other. Our souls will never be separated." He spoke in a small tender voice that I had never heard before. Together, we pulled close to each other. That night, after putting the children to bed, we walked on the beach into the early morning. On the beach, we held each other tightly and skirted the oncoming waves with our bare feet. At times we just looked seaward, and I thought of him in harms way with no power to protect him.

The wind suddenly increased with a steady sharply, meeting my fragile body with a decisive blow that gave me a sense of destiny and purpose for being there at this point and time. When he left that day, I felt a strange closeness that I had never experienced before. In my mind and soul, I knew that he was right in what he had said. For that reason, I was closer to him then than on the first night we made love. A month later, I felt the movement in my lower abdomen. I was pregnant again, this time with his fourth child. Instinctively I knew and wrote him that the child would be a boy, and I would name the child after him. He was gone longer than his usual tour of duty, some thirteen months.

On returning, he was a different man inside. His eyes were different. They had the look of fear and pain that was not there before. From the naval base I had heard of the horror and the futility of the battles they had fought; women and children were the enemy, not just ordinary soldiers. No one could tell if the people that they were fighting for were friend or foe. I had to respect his right to his pain and his frustration that he was experiencing. If he needed me, I would be there for him. Otherwise, our relationship was not worth the time we had spent together.

In the distance, I could see lightning showing the outline of the massive thunderheads of a major storm approaching the shoreline. This was where the approaching gusting wind was coming from. The force reminded me of the gentle forcefulness of his body tenderly pressing against my soft body when we had made love. With age, his body grew in broadness and manliness so that, at times, it was solid and as immovable as granite. I loved to lay my cheek on his hard hairy chest. With his deep breathing, I could feel the power that lay dormant in his beautiful body. A smile appeared on my lips. When we made love for the first time he had only one or two hairs on his broad chest, I remembered while the strong, forceful wind caressed my fragile body as I stepped into the wind and the oncoming waves.

I could remember after his tour in Vietnam he transferred to the Pentagon where the promotions came to him quickly. I could never understand how that worked. This is a business after all, and he had his job to do while I had mine.

I had heard rumors, through my naval contacts, that he was being groomed to be an Admiral. I only wanted him to be happy doing what he wanted to do with his life. I was busy now getting the children married and then having grandchildren.

The gushing wind from the storm was creating white caps - a foot in height. The smile on my lips suddenly disappeared. During our walks near to the last, he started to talk about the Phantom Jets that he loved and the war that he had been a part of. He did not like the new faster jets. They were too fast and complicated to fly and to keep up with. The Phantoms were versatile and could fly fast. They made it easier for a man to fly by the seat of his pants. They could be patched up with simple gear and baling wire if needed. With the new fighters, a system could go down, and it might take a couple of minutes or three weeks to make the plane flyable again. When he started to talk about the war, I could see the tears forming in this great man's eyes. I had only seen him cry three times;

at each of his parent's funeral, and when he held his son for the first time. He was a man made to follow orders, even if it meant destroying an entire village of women and children. He had the obligation to the men who followed him to justify our actions in this war. I still could remember the disillusionment in his voice that evening. "It was a political war. Our hands were tied at every turn and every time we were ready to destroy the real enemy; we were not allowed to. I'm not a political fighter. I'm only a Naval Officer, who only follows orders," he said in a solemn, and subdued voice that I could barely hear over the surf.

He was gone for several months after he had told me this confession of his pain and agony that dwelled inside him. The reason for his departure was not told to me. He simply said, "I have to tend to some naval business for a couple of months. I'll write you every week. Take care of the kids. Remember I love you. This was his business for the country that he served and not my business to know where he was going. At the time, I was overwhelmed with grandchildren.

In the distance, I could see the thunder cloud moving in closer and the lighting striking more often. One day in late fall he came home early from the Naval Base. He told me that the Admiral had wanted him to command a new flight wing in the Pacific and that he was being considered for the promotion of Vice-Admiral. I noticed that he was troubled in telling me this.

During our evening walk on the seashore, he informed me that he would be retiring when he came back from this Pacific tour. He would turn down the opportunity that the Admiral had offered him. He turned to me and held my hands and spoke so softly that I could barely hear him speak. "I want to spend time with you. I've missed you when I've been away. The flying makes me miss you more." We walked together that evening only holding hands and stopping, intimately staring out into the vast ocean. That night while I slept, he cradled my fragile body on his chest.

In the morning, I made him a simple breakfast of black coffee, toast, and fried eggs sunny-side up. Halfway through the meal, he placed his large coffee cup on the small oak table and looked for a long period of time into my green eyes. He gently spoke in a serious, tone directly to my inner being. "Don't worry. I'll be back. No man would want to be away from a beautiful woman like me. This is the reason that I've come back Toto you every time." His words scared me. I didn't want him to leave my side again. This time was similar to when he left on his first tour of Vietnam. I could not say anything for this was his decision of what to do in his life, not mine. If he wanted my input, he would ask me.

I turned back to the oncoming wind, which pushed my body slightly. The cold wind reminded me of the cold winter morning that first day of March. There was a fine, thin coat of snow on the ground and the sidewalk that led up to our cottage in DC. I looked at the two Naval Captains who had left a trail of footprints as they walked to the front door of the cottage. They did not have to say anything. He was not coming home. They told me that he was just missing in a training exercise off the coast of Korea and that he would probably be found in the next 24 hours. The look behind our eyes told me this was not the truth. He was lost at sea, never to return.

I turned abruptly into the wind, which pressed against my wide hips and small bosom. "He said that he would return. He was always a man of his word", I thought, feeling the emptiness and the pain of missing him for the past years. "He was different from other men!" I spoke; sending my voice loudly into the total darkness that lay before me above the roaring waves that crashed in front of me.

Turning toward the beach house, I thought of the grandchildren. It was time for them to go to bed. 'Maybe I will take them on the porch and tell them about our grandfather and explain to them that he was a man among men, that men respected and followed. I'll let them feel the power of the wind that he traveled on when he flew the Phantoms.

I felt an emptiness inside my soul as I walked toward the beach house porch. There was a feeling of completeness within me. The completeness was his love, letting me free to love him and grow with him. My small, delicate smile returned to my face as I climbed the porch steps. "Maybe he won't come tomorrow evening, but he is always with me." I reached the porch landing and turned one more time to watch the storm approaching and the violent waves along the seashore.

"No man would ever replace him." He was correct when he had told me that a long time ago, that …"We would always be next to each other's hearts". "Our souls would never be apart and never separated from each other." I thought of this while turning toward the porch screen door. I could feel the wetness starting to touch my soft cheek.

The Vigil

A person stands alone in a Vigil for love to be fulfilled.
Yet, in their body and soul, there is completeness in this
  Vigil.
Their love was never separated when they were together.
Now, they are separated, and their love can still be separated.

Each has given all to the other.
Each heart still beats with each other's.
Each one can still feel the others breathe on their skin
  in the quite of the evening.
Each heart longs for the sight of their love.

They will always long for each other's touch.
They will never leave each others grasp.

They have given to each other asking nothing in return.
They have let their love flee and be free to find their own
  path.
Love has become stronger and more enduring.

The bond of love will never be broken even in death.
Love will exist for each other for eternity.
Love will hold the Vigil every moment until the two
  become one again.